PIECES OF A SPIRAL

Volume 6

By Kaimu Tachibana

CONTENTS

CAST OF CHARACTERS

PIECES OF A SPIRAL

....
RUKI
...

CLENCH

LET'S TAKE IT OUT-SIDE.
WE CAN'T FIGHT IT OUT IN HERE... NOT WITH MAGIC.
HMPH...
IF YOU WISH.
GLANCE
...
RUKI?

FAWOOOSH

RUKI!!
SAJO!
TAGI!?
FOOSH
HUH ?!

DEMONS!
HUFF HUFF
MAN, THOSE IDI-OTS!
THERE'S NO WAY THOSE TWO CAN TAKE OUT SAJO!
HEEEY ...

WAKYO, WE COULD BACK 'EM UP!
......
UGH ...
WAKYO! ARE YOU OKAY?
AGH ...
....
SAJO... DAMN HIM ...!

SA-KUYA ...
YOU MUST TEND TO WAKYO'S WOUND QUICKLY.
BESIDES, YOUR INJURY FROM THAT MIRROR FRAGMENT STILL ISN'T FULLY HEALED.
YOUR PRIORITY HAS TO BE GETTING WELL.

YOU'LL NEVER BE ABLE TO VANQUISH SAJO UNLESS YOU'RE BOTH ONE-HUNDRED PERCENT.
B-BUT... BISHU-SAMA ...

......
I SAID NO. RIGHT NOW, WE HAVE NO CHOICE BUT TO LEAVE THE FIGHT TO HIM--
HIM--?

OR MAYBE I SHOULD SAY, *"THEM"* ...
...
TSK! *WHERE DID THEY GO?!*
FLAPPA FLAPPA
FIND THEM.

DON'T FAIL ME.
... BISHU?
WHY CAN'T YOU COME TO ME...
I'VE COME ALL THIS WAY TO KEEP MY PROMISE, AFTER ALL...
MAN, IT'S TAKING A LONG TIME TO HEAL.
WELL, IT'S ONE NASTY-ASS WOUND.

RUKI ...
SIGH.
...HE JUST WANTS TO GET SAJO AS FAR AWAY FROM THE HOSPITAL-- FROM US--AS POSSIBLE.
FINE-- I'M GOING AFTER THEM!
WE CAN'T JUST ABANDON THEM TO SAJO--WE GOTTA HELP THEM!

MY WOUND -- IT'S OKAY NOW.
I WANT TO GO, TOO, BISHU-SAMA!

THERE ARE HUMANS WHO REACH OUT TO DEMONS--

JUST AS THERE ARE DEMONS WHO YEARN TO BE WITH HUMANS.

AGH!
CLUTCH
WHAT THE --?!
THUMP
WELL DONE, SHIKI-GAMI!

SHIKI-GAMI ?!
WE CAN'T HAVE YOU WANDERING AROUND LOOSE HERE IN THE HUMAN REALM, NOW CAN WE?
?!
DEMON... YOU CAN RUN BUT YOU CAN'T HIDE.
A-AN ONMYO SORCERER --?!

RUSTLE
RUSTLE
WELL, WELL, WHAT HAVE WE HERE?
I MUST SAY, I'VE NEVER HAD A DEMON GIVE ME THIS MUCH TROUBLE BEFORE.

ARE THOSE VIO-LET EYES?
UGH, JUST LOOKING AT THEM MAKES MY SKIN CRAWL.
!!
AGGH!!

THUMP
ARGH --!!
HEY, THAT HURT! WHAT'S THE MATTER WITH YOU!!
....

RRRRRRRRRRRR

IT'S **BAD** TO HARM OR KILL HUMANS-- 'CAUSE IT JUST MAKES THINGS **HARD** FOR US.
YEAH, BUT **LOOK** WHAT THEY DID TO MY **EYES**.
AN **ONMYO SORCERER** DID THAT-- USED HIS **MAGIC** ON YOU.
THAT'S HOW THEY **ARE**-- THEY **HATE DEMONS**.
DO **YOU** HATE HUMANS, TAGI?
KINDA...

ME, TOO!
BUT THE ONE WHO HELPED YOU-- HE'S A REAL WEIRDO.
STILL, SOME HUMANS ARE NICE.
....

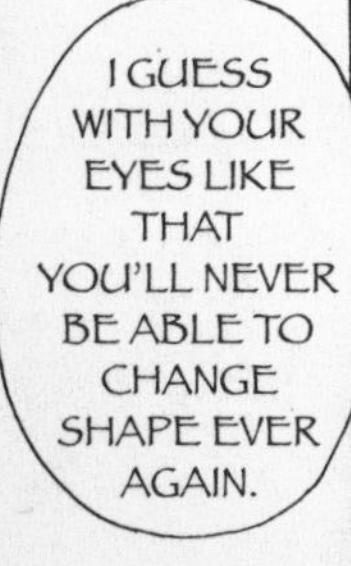
I GUESS WITH YOUR EYES LIKE THAT YOU'LL NEVER BE ABLE TO CHANGE SHAPE EVER AGAIN.

HEY, IT'S THAT LITTLE GIRL. THE HUMAN YOU PLAY WITH?
AREN'T YOU GONNA SEE HER? --SHE'S CALLING FOR YOU.
NO!
I WON'T ...
I WON'T GO ...
EVEN WITH THESE RAVAGED EYES, I SEE HER.
OYUKI-CHAAAN --

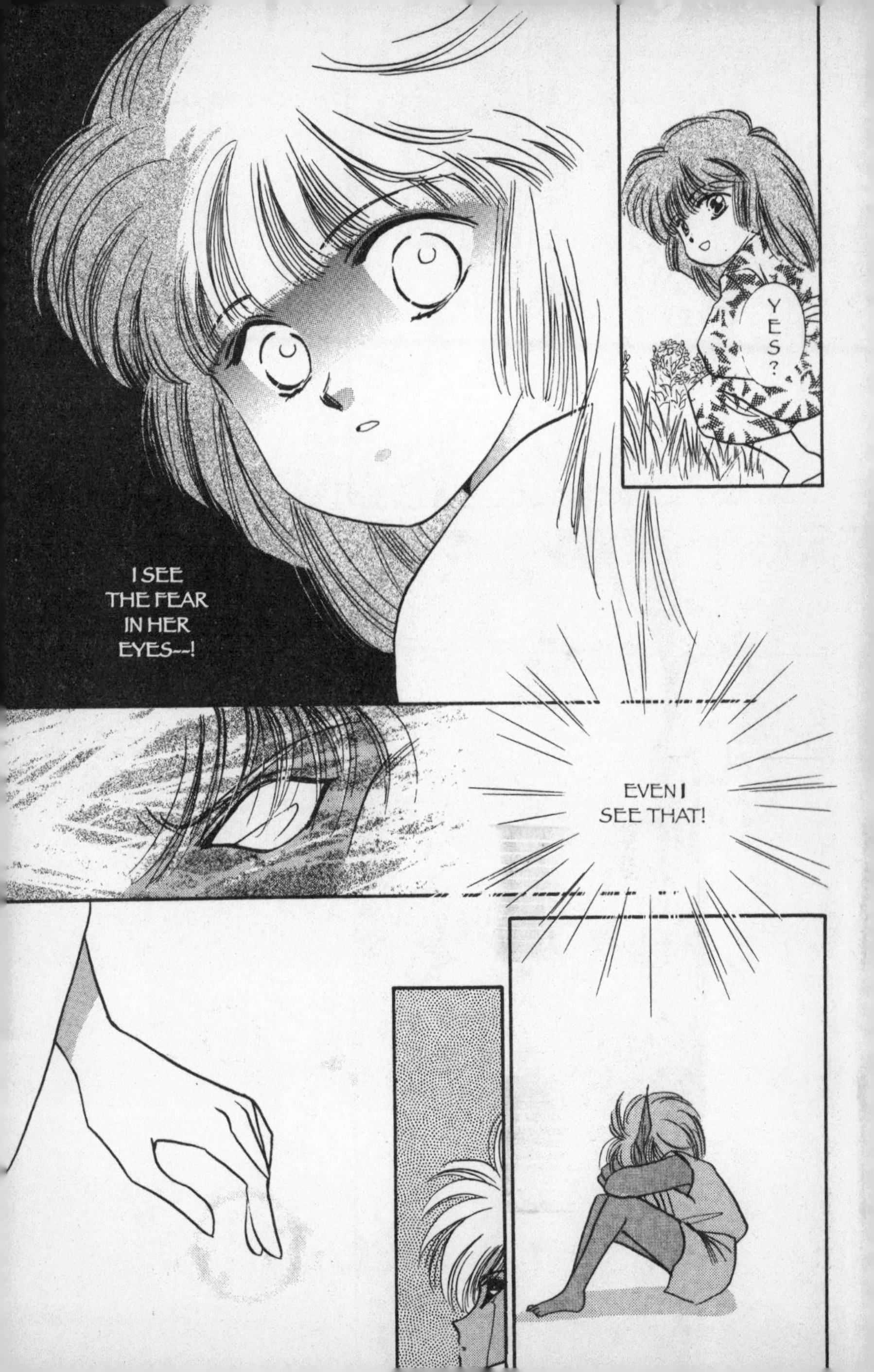
YES?
I SEE THE FEAR IN HER EYES--!
EVEN I SEE THAT!

OH, BISHU-SAMA!
THAT'S BISHU'S MARK --
YOU ...!
YOU'RE A FRIEND OF BISHU'S, AREN'T YOU?
FWIT
FLINCH

SO, WHERE'D THE OTHER TWO GO?
BISHU'S FRIENDS?
......
MAYBE ALL THAT STUFF BEFORE WAS ONMYO SORCERY--
HOW DO YOU KNOW BISHU-SAMA?
AND THE SHIKI-GAMI ...WHAT ARE YOU, AN ONMYO SOR-CERESS?!
DON'T BE SILLY, I'M JUST A COLLEGE GIRL.
HE JUST SHOWED ME A FEW TRICKS, THAT'S ALL.
ONMYO SORCERY'S JUST LEFT OVER FROM MY LAST LIFE.
HUH? LAST LIFE --?!

AND NOW I'M HERE TO MAKE GOOD ON MY PROMISE TO BISHU.
....
SHOOO
GULP
PROMISE?
AND YOU-- YOU KNOW WHERE BISHU IS DON'T YOU...?
TAGI! COME QUICK!!
?!
RUKI?!

THINK YOU CAN TAKE ME ON WITH THAT HOLE IN YOUR FORE-HEAD?
COULD YOU BE ANY MORE STUPID?
AT LEAST I'M HONORING THE PRINCIPLES OF THE THREE-EYE FACTION.
IS THAT SO?
AS FOR WHICH OF US IS MORE STUPID ...

NOW'S YOUR BIG CHANCE.
HUH?
C'MON, WHAT'RE YOU WAITING FOR?

DO I HAVE TO SPELL IT OUT FOR YOU? YOUR HABITATION TRICK--DO IT FOR ME.
...PATHETIC. IS THAT THE BEST YOU CAN DO?
YOU THINK THAT DESPERATE TACTIC WILL HELP YOU WIN?
OR ARE YOU DEFECT-ING TO THE WINNING SIDE?
I'M SERIOUS.
EVEN IF IT'S NOT PERFECT WHEN YOU GET INTO MASAYUKI, IT'LL BE GOOD ENOUGH TO FOOL THEM.

ANYWAY, I WANT TO TEST YOUR STRENGTH.
BECAUSE I DON'T THINK YOU POSSESS ME.
YOU HAVEN'T LEARNED A THING, HAVE YOU...?
WHERE DID YOU GET THIS OBNOXIOUS COCKINESS?
WHERE, YOU ASK?
I'M YOUR SUCCESSOR, AREN'T I?
YES, TRUE...

BUT JUST WHAT IS YOUR ANGLE --?
DO YOU TRULY JUST WANT TO KNOW WHO'S STRONGER?
EXACTLY!
GO! DO IT NOW!
HM, I DON'T THINK I WANT TO PLAY YOUR LITTLE GAME.
!
BETTER TO KILL YOU FIRST AND THEN INHABIT YOU.

SUIT YOURSELF, MAKES NO DIFFERENCE TO ME.
HMPH.
TAGI! HURRY !!
!!

ZZZZT
?!
ZZZZTSSST
UGH!
WHAT ... GIVES ...?
THOUGHT YOU WERE... GONNA... *KILL* ME *FIRST* ...
LIKE A *SPIDER* WITH ITS *PREY*-- I'LL KILL YOU WHEN I'M *READY*.

FZZZT
A ... AGH --
BUT FIRST, YOU'LL SHOW ME WHAT TRICKS YOU'VE GOT UP YOUR SLEEVE, RUKI!
TAGI, WHERE ARE YOU?!
RUKI!!
TAGI!

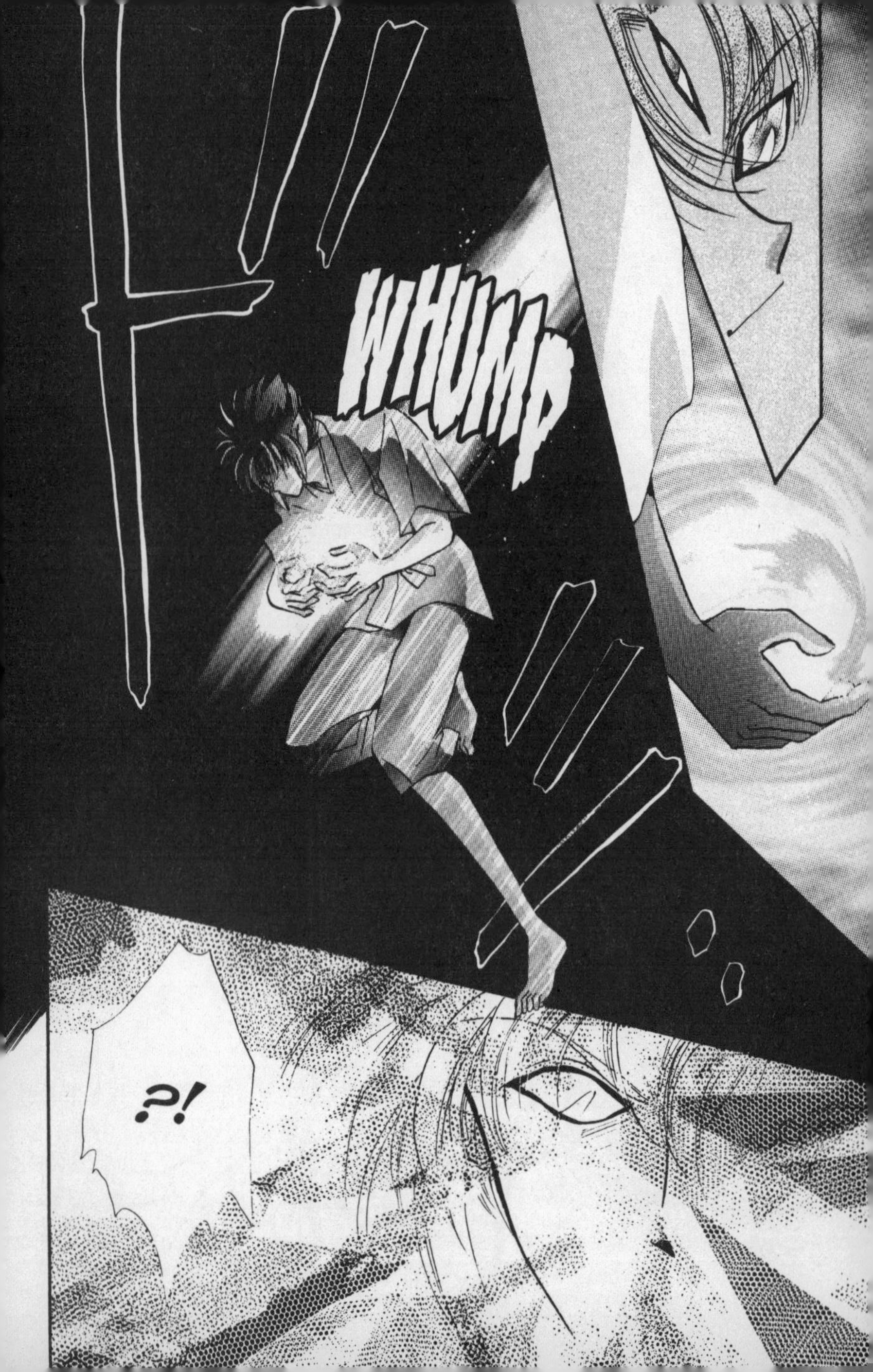
WHUMP
?!

WHAT'S GOING ON?! TELL ME!!
RU ... RŪKI ...

PLOP PLOP PLOP
RUKI --!!
THUMP

RUKI !!
RUKI !!
WHAT'S HAP- PENED TO YOU?!

TA ... TAGI ...
BEFORE HE TAKES CONTROL ...
YOU MUST ...
TH... THERE'S STILL TIME ...
STOP BABBLING! YOUR WOUNDS --!!

LIS-TEN TO ME--!
...RUKI ?!
HE'S IN ME--NOW'S OUR CHANCE...!
KILL ME...!
DO IT, TAGI! FINISH ME OFF!!

IF YOU DO IT...
I CAN BEAT HIM... SAJO, LORD OF THE THREE-EYE FACTION ...!!
TAGI!!
DO IT!!
I-I CAN'T !!
TAGI !!
IT'S NOT THAT EASY!

HOW CAN YOU ASK ME TO DO THIS?! IT'S NOT SO SIMPLE, RUKI ...!
TAGI ...

......

NO...OF COURSE NOT ...

DROP

RUKI ...
YOUR LITTLE SCHEME IS DESTINED TO FAIL, RUKI--
?!
SA-SAJO ?!
RISE
YOU FOOLS WILL NEVER LEARN!

RU ... RUKI ...
UGH
RUKI ?!
WHAAM!!
WHAT'S MINE IS YOURS, TAGI!!

WITH MY EYES YOU SHALL SEE, TAGI!
RUKI ?!

DON'T LET ME DOWN ...
RUKI ?
TAGI ...
AH ...!

RUKI ?!

RUKI!
RUKI !!
C'MON ...!
RUKI !!

OPEN YOUR EYES!
LOOK AT ME, RUKI!

HE NO LONGER HAS EYES, TAGI...
NOW THEY'RE YOUR VIOLET EYES.
I DON'T WANT THEM! MAKE HIM TAKE THEM BACK!
WAP
YOU GAVE ME YOUR EYES --WHY?! SO I COULD SEE YOU LIKE THIS?!
RUKI!

I'VE ONLY MADE IT THIS FAR BECAUSE OF YOU!
YOU MADE IT POSSIBLE FOR ME TO LIVE... EVEN WITHOUT SIGHT...

I...
I...

STOP IT! I CAN'T BEAR TO FEEL THEIR TEARS...!!

YOU'VE SHOWN ME MORE THAN I DARED HOPE, RUKI.
A SPLENDID PERFORMANCE, MIGHT I ADD.
NOTHING MORE THAN MY DUTY AS A MEMBER OF THE THREE-EYE FACTION.
SAJO... FOR BISHU-SAMA'S SAKE LET ME DIE HERE.
DIE... FOR BISHU'S SAKE?
ONLY A FOOL THROWS AWAY HIS OWN LIFE.
AND TO DIE BEFORE YOUR LORD'S OWN DEATH IS THE ULTIMATE BETRAYAL.

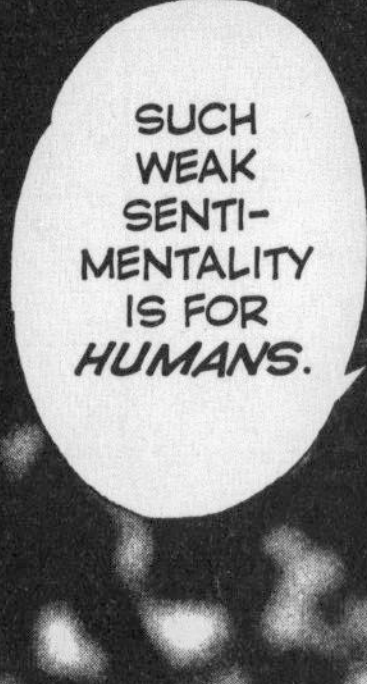
MAYBE YOU JUST DON'T UNDERSTAND WHAT IT MEANS TO SACRIFICE YOURSELF.
SUCH WEAK SENTIMENTALITY IS FOR HUMANS.

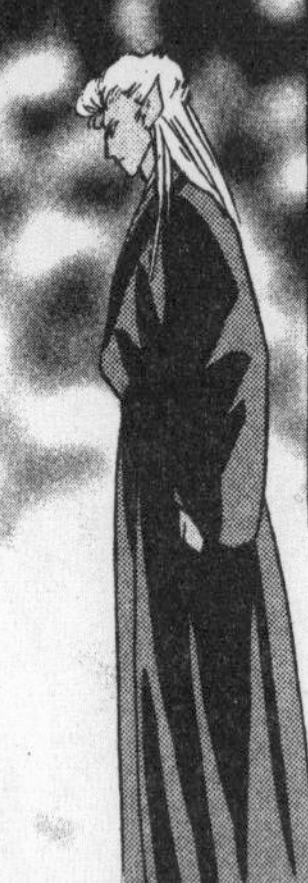
THAT'S WHERE YOU AND I DISAGREE.

I DON'T THINK WE'RE DIFFERENT AT ALL.

WE'RE EXACTLY THE SAME.
WE'RE DE-MONS ...
BUT THE HUMANS -- THEY'RE JUST DIFFER-ENT ...
......
......

TAKE ME WITH YOU, SAJO.
FAINT

I AM THE LORD OF THE THREE EYE FAC-TION.

YOU...

AND I WILL FULFILL MY DESTINY.

...WILL FULFILL YOUR DESTINY...

AAAHHH

....
HACK
YOU ARE A PERFECT FOOL, RUKI.
YOU THINK YOU'RE WORTHY TO FOLLOW IN MY FOOTSTEPS?

RUKI... NO!!
I DON'T *WANT* TO SEE!
?!
WHY ARE YOU DOING THIS?
I DON'T WANT TO *WATCH YOU SUFFER* LIKE THIS!

SAJO!!
WHAT ARE YOU GRINNING ABOUT, HUH?!
RUKI SACRIFICED HIMSELF FOR YOU... YOU!!
ENOUGH DRAMA. IT'S ONLY A MEANINGLESS DEATH IN THE HUMAN REALM.

THE BOY WAS SIMPLY *TOO STUPID TO LIVE*, IF YOU ASK *ME*.
GRRR ...!
EZZZT
WHAAM
WHAT'S *THIS?* YOU'LL NEED MORE THAN *VIOLET EYES* TO VANQUISH *ME!*
YOUR *FOOL-HARDI-NESS* TRULY *AMAZES* ME!

I...
WILL ...
CRUSH YOU, SAJO!!
KAARAAK
?!
RRRUUUMBLE
KSSHH
PLUNK

NOT BAD... FOR YOU, ANY-WAY ...
NOW WATCH THE MAS-TER.
YOU HAVE A DEATH WISH ?
HAPPY TO OBLIGE !
HOW DARE YOU CHAL-LENGE ME?!
I'LL SHOW YOU THAT THIS IS NO SCHOOL-BOY GAME!
KARAAK
!!
FOOOM

WHY'RE YOU STICKING UP FOR HIM, MAYUKO ?!
HE'S ONE OF THEM-- A DEMON!
SHUT UP AND STAY PUT!
FWIT
IT VIOLATES MY SENSE OF FAIR PLAY...
I CAN'T JUST STAND BY AND WATCH HIM SUFFER HELPLESSLY UNDER THE THUMB OF THAT SADIST.
GET OUTTA THE WAY !!
HEY!
I'M NOT HELPLESS!
BUMP
MAN, YOU REALLY DO HAVE A DEATH WISH ...!
YOU ...?
...THE OTHER DAY... YES, THE ONMYO SORCERY!

HMPH
NOW THIS *WILL* BE A *PLEASURE.*
I CAN'T THANK YOU ENOUGH.

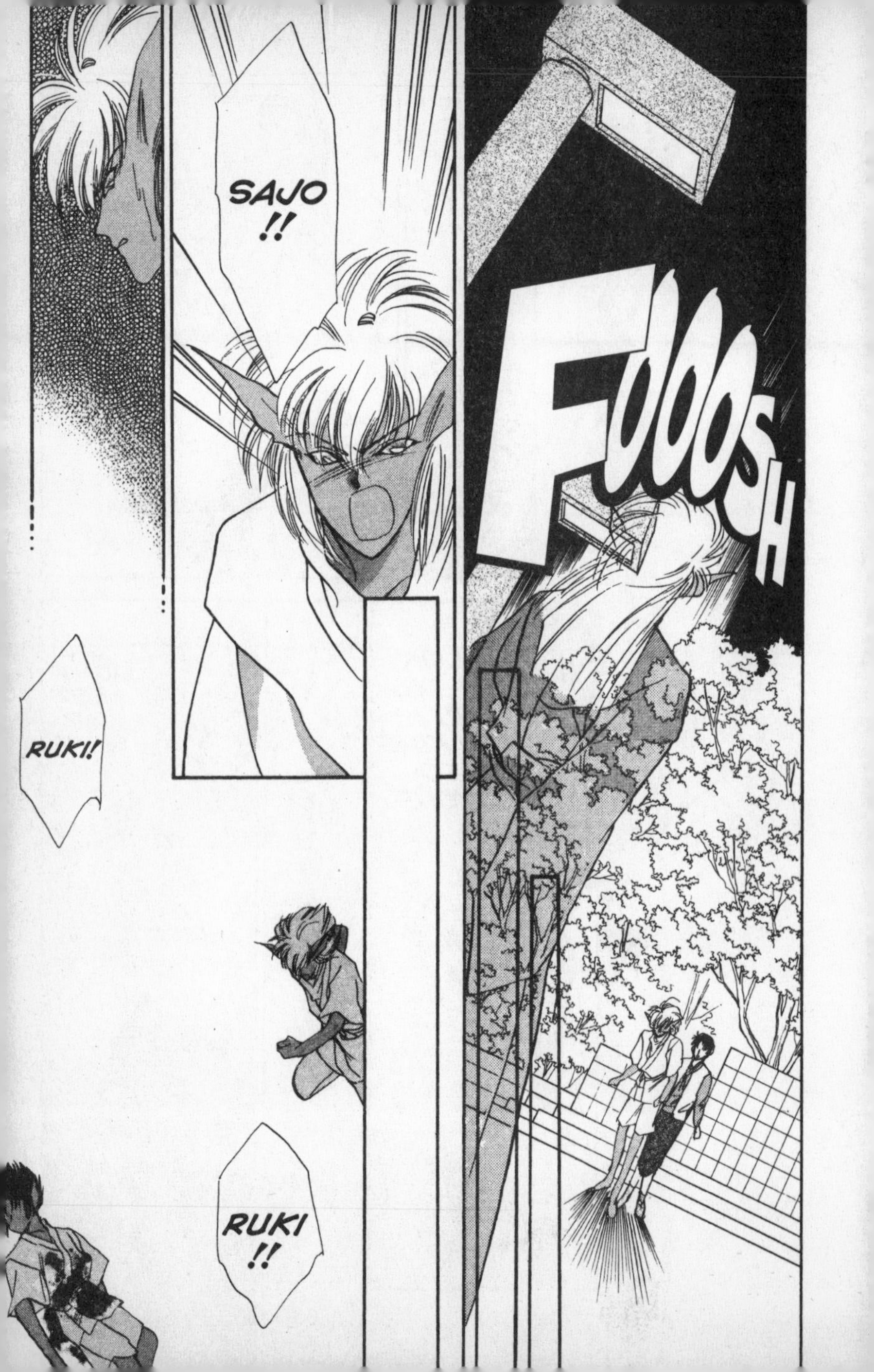
FOOOSH
SAJO!!
RUKI!!
...
RUKI!

IDIOT! WHERE DO YOU GET OFF TRYING TO BE SUCH A HERO?!
I'LL NEVER FORGIVE YOU FOR THIS-- NEVER!
DAMMIT, RUKI... LISTEN TO ME!!
I DON'T NEED YOUR SIGHT...
...SO I'M GIVING IT BACK.
LOOK AT ME, I'M TALKING TO YOU!
RUKI...
RUKI!!

SAJO ...
HE WON'T GET AWAY WITH THIS ...
RUKI ...

....
WELL, WELL...I *KNEW* YOU'D TURN UP *SOONER* OR *LATER* ...
BISHU.

HEY ...
WHERE ARE YOU GOING?
HEY! I SAID ...
SHUT UP!
WHY DON'T YOU JUST LEAVE US ALONE!

FOOOSH

WHAT'S THE *MATTER* WITH YOU? *GO AFTER HIM.*

DON'T BE *RIDICU-LOUS* ...
HE JUST *WATCHED* HIS *FRIEND DIE.*

DON'T TELL ME YOU'RE CRYING! IF IT WAS A HUMAN, FINE, BUT WE'RE TALKING ABOUT A DEMON HERE...
SO WHAT ?!
YOU KNOW, I REALLY, REALLY HATE THAT ABOUT YOU!
....

RUKI, WE'RE HERE.
THE FOREST... WHERE WE USED TO PLAY ALL THE TIME.
IT'S COMPLETELY DIFFERENT NOW, THOUGH.

LOOK, RUKI.
THAT'S THE TREE.
REMEMBER? THE ONE WE'D ALWAYS CLIMB.
I COULDN'T SEE, BUT YOU'D DESCRIBE IT ALL ...
WE'D SIT THERE AND WATCH THE HUMANS DOWN BELOW.
THANKS TO YOU, I DID SEE. YOU WERE MY EYES.

RUKI...
YOUR LAST WORDS...
DON'T WORRY, I'LL NEVER FOR-GET.
...I'LL WATCH OVER THEM... TO THE VERY END...

.....
YOUR EYES... I REALLY WASN'T MEANT TO HAVE THEM.
THEY ACHE ...

...AND THEY'RE *ALWAYS* *FULL OF* *TEARS*.

WHAT, SAKU-YA?
I DUNNO... I FELT SOMETHING... LIKE RUKI, MAYBE--
NAAH... PROBABLY JUST MY IMAGINATION.
HOW DID YOU FIND ME?
I KNOW YOU DON'T YET HAVE THE ABILITY ...
IT WAS SAJO.
HE TOLD ME YOU WERE HERE.

I TOLD HIM I REALLY NEEDED TO SEE MY FATHER.
HEH
HMPH, YOUR FILIAL CONCERN IS MOST TOUCHING.
BUT THE TRUTH IS... I REALLY DID WANT TO SEE YOU.
REALLY.
YOU EXPECT ME TO BELIEVE THAT, WHEN YOU'VE ONLY EVER SHUNNED ME?

I COULDN'T BRING MYSELF TO *KILL* YOU.
IT *BOTHERED* ME FOR THE *LONGEST TIME*.
FOR A TIME YOU *PRETENDED* TO BE A *KIND* AND *LOVING FATHER*.
DURING THAT HAPPY INTERLUDE I *LEARNED* WHAT IT MEANT TO BE *HUMAN*.
YOU SEARED THAT MOMENT OF HAPPINESS *INDELIBLY* INTO MY MEMORY.
AND *THEN* ...

"YOU KILLED MOTHER."
"WILL YOU KILL FATHER, TOO?"
"HOW COLD-BLOODED AND CRUEL "HUMANS" ARE..."
YOU SAID THOSE THINGS. YOU SAID THEM TO YOUR SON, WHO SO YEARNED TO BE HUMAN, AND YOU MADE HIM A PRISONER OF YOUR FEAR.

TELL SAJO.
TELL HIM THAT INCITING MY WRATH WILL NOT STOP THIS...
MASAYUKI IS NOT THE WEAK LINK THAT WILL BRING DOWN SAKUYA AND WAKYO.
HE IS THE SOLID ROCK ON WHICH THEY STAND.

SO NOW YOU KNOW *TIME IS RUNNING OUT*.
SOON WE'LL BE ON THE *FINAL* STAGE.
AND YOU KNOW THERE IS NOTHING YOU CAN DO TO STOP IT.
FATHER.

BISHU.
BEING HUMAN... HOW DOES IT FEEL?

THERE IS NO GREATER BLESSING, NO GREATER JOY.

INDEED.
AND THAT IS YOUR WEAK-NESS.
BISHU ...
YOU KNOW, AT THIS MOMENT, I ACTUALLY FEEL GRATE-FUL.
YOU FINALLY FOUND SOME REASON TO VALUE ME.

MOTHER, ARE YOU HAPPY TO BE AT YOUR HUSBAND'S SIDE...
...HAVING BECOME A DEMON YOUR-SELF?

YOUR UNFATHOM-ABLE SORROW, MOTHER, IS ALL THAT I CARRY OF YOU WITHIN ME NOW.

IS IT WISE TO JUST LET HIM GO!
GO AHEAD, HAVE YOUR SAY WHILE I'M TRAPPED HERE IN THIS INFERNAL PURGA-TORY.
AH, SAJO. YOU'VE RETURNED.
REST ASSURED, HIS TWO LITTLE FOLLOWERS WILL GO DOWN WITH HIM WHEN HE FALLS...
YES, MY LORD.
OH, YES? I'M SO GLAD.

HOLD IT, YOU TWO!

GAH!!
YOU ...!
THE OMYOJI!

IT'S MAYUKO, IF YOU DON'T MIND. HOW ABOUT NOT IGNORING ME FOR JUST A SECOND ?
YOU KNOW, YOU BOTH MAKE A PRETTY MISER-ABLE BISHU.

THAT
WHA...? WHAT ARE YOU TALKING ABOUT ...
DOES BISHU HAVE THAT ON HIS FORE-HEAD? NO!
WHICH MEANS THAT YOU TWO ARE NOT BISHU.
BISHU CAN TWIST DEMONS AROUND HIS LITTLE FINGER. HE DOESN'T NEED SOMETHING LIKE THAT TO PROTECT HIM.

YOU TWO ARE NOTHING BUT RANK AMATEURS, IF YOU ASK ME.
YOU'RE LUCKY BISHU'S GOT YOUR BACK.
WHO ASKED YOU ?!

HA! SEE?
BISHU WOULD NEVER POP OFF LIKE THAT!

WHERE, OH WHERE, COULD THE REAL BISHU BE...?
SIGH

WHO IS THIS ONMYOJI, ANYWAY ...?
LOOK, WE DON'T HAVE TIME FOR YOUR GAMES RIGHT NOW!

YOU'RE LOOKING FOR RUKI AND TAGI, RIGHT?

?!

AND JUST WHAT DO YOU KNOW ABOUT THEM?!
UH...
I... IT'S KIND OF *HARD* TO *EXPLAIN*...

WELL, START TRYING... *NOW!*
YANK

ALL RIGHT, ALL RIGHT, I'LL *TELL* YOU! NOW *LET GO!*
....
THIS... THIS *ISN'T EASY* TO SAY...

RUKI'S
DEAD.

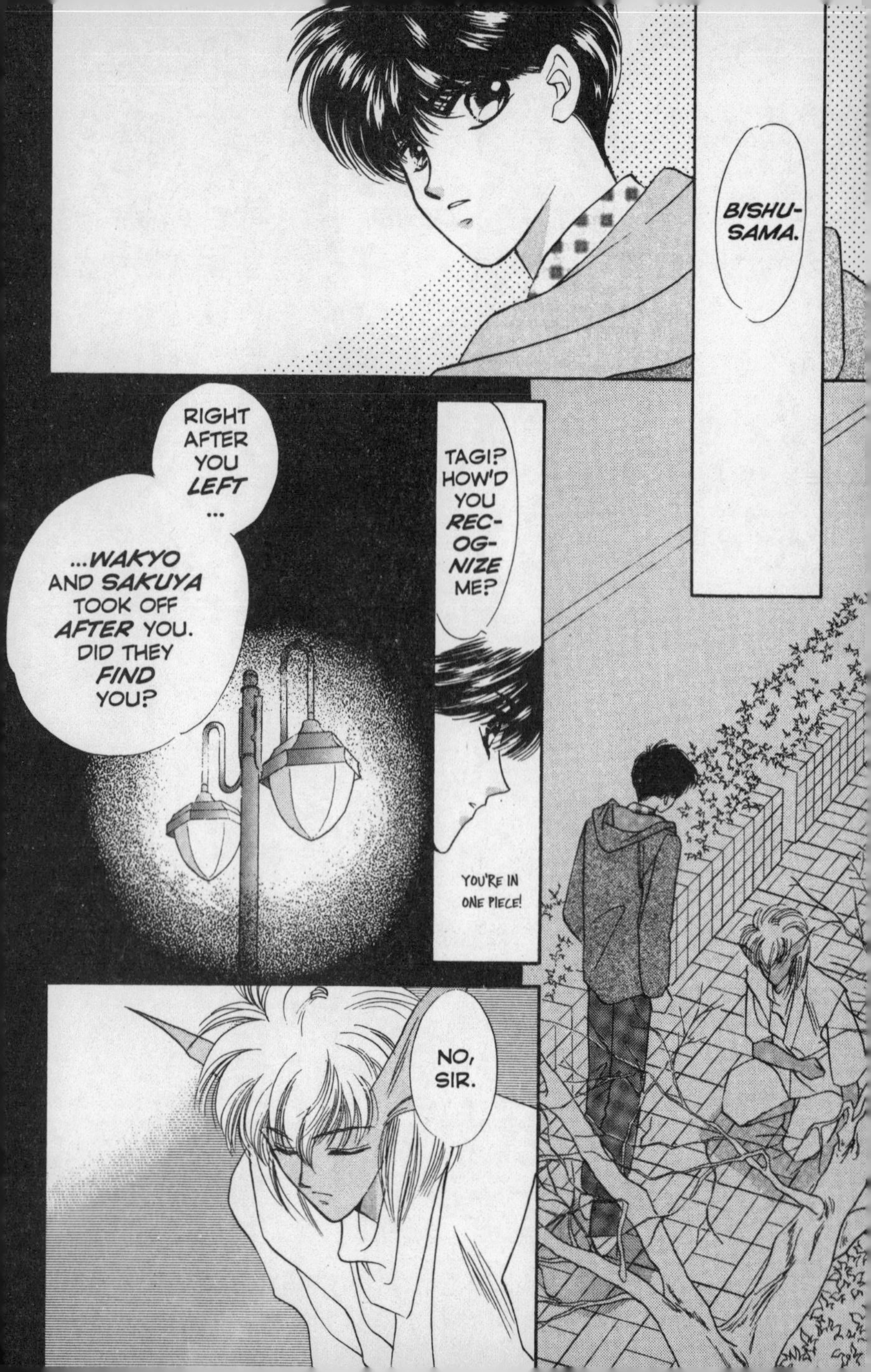
BISHU-SAMA.
TAGI? HOW'D YOU RECOG-NIZE ME?
YOU'RE IN ONE PIECE!
RIGHT AFTER YOU LEFT ...
...WAKYO AND SAKUYA TOOK OFF AFTER YOU. DID THEY FIND YOU?
NO, SIR.

AND RUKI? WHERE'S HE?

BISHU-SAMA ...
RUKI, HE'S ...

OH, BISHU-SAMA ...

..I SEE.
NOW RUKI HAS BECOME A PART OF YOU...
TAGI.
...Y...
...YES, BISHU-SAMA.

BISHU-SAMA ...
HE HAS.
TAGI ...

YOU LIE-- RUKI'S NOT DEAD!
SAJO ?!
OR MAYBE YOU KILLED HIM!
GIMME A BREAK, WHY WOULD *I* KILL HIM?!
BECAUSE I WAS AN *ONMYOJI* IN THE *LAST WORLD* ?!
WAP
SA-KUYA!
DON'T BE STUPID!

THAT DEMON IN BLACK WITH THE THREE VIOLET EYES KILLED HIM!
SA ... SAJO ...
THEN SAJO... SAJO MURDERED RUKI ...
SAJO !!
CLENCH
SO NOW DO YOU BELIEVE ME? I ONLY WANT TO HONOR MY WORD.
BELIEVE ME, I WOULDN'T BE HERE IF I DIDN'T HAVE TO BE.

I KNOW YOU... YOU'VE *SHADOWED* BISHU-SAMA FOR A LONG TIME...FROM *BEFORE* THE LAST WORLD.
YOU'RE AFTER BISHU-SAMA'S LIFE, THAT'S WHAT YOU *WANT*...!
THAT'S RIGHT. *I KEEP MY PROMISES.*

BISHU ...
WHEN THE TIME COMES ...

I'LL DO IT.
I'LL KILL YOU WITH THESE HANDS.

LOOK OVER THERE-- IT'S WHERE THE **HUMANS** LIVE!
BISHU-SAMA!

DEMONS ...?!
EVEN HERE.... IN THIS VILLAGE?!

BISHU-SAMA, ARE YOU COMING?
I'LL BE RIGHT THERE.
NO, NOT DEMONS ...
SHIKIGAMI!!!

AND THERE'S THE ONE THEY SERVE AND PROTECT...THE NEMESIS OF ALL DEMONS, LORD AND UNDERLING ALIKE...
AN ON-MYOJI ...
BISHU-SAMA, ARE YOU OKAY?
GLANCE
....
W... WAKYO ....!
STARE

I'M FINE! NOW, LET'S GET GOING.
YOU SURE...?
LOOK!
THERE HE IS AGAIN!
I THOUGHT SO...I SAW HIM BEFORE! HE IS FOLLOWING US!
WHAT DOES HE WANT? WHY DOESN'T HE JUST COME AND TALK TO US?

HE'S ONLY INTERESTED IN **ME**.

ONLY ME...

I'M A DEMON... DOES HE INTEND TO KILL ME?

PFFF
I'VE NEVER SEEN A DEMON LIKE HIM.
HE LOOKS EXACTLY LIKE A HUMAN.
EXCEPT FOR ONE THING... THE VIOLET EYES.

HE IS THE CHILD OF THE DEMON LORD, GARAI.
YOU GOT A SCAR...
ON YOUR ARM...AND ON YOUR STOMACH, TOO.
THIS? IT'S FROM A LONG TIME AGO, FROM A FIGHT WITH A POWERFUL DEMON LORD.
A DEMON, REALLY? AND A LORD, TOO?!
WOW
I WAS RESCUING A CHILD...
ANYWAY, IT WAS A LONG TIME AGO.

IT'S NOTHING TO GET **WORKED UP** ABOUT.
....

DEMON CHILDREN ARE HIDEOUSLY UGLY.
JUST LOOK AT THIS VERMIN HERE...
BUT **HE** LOOKS HUMAN. HE EVEN HAS A **HUMAN CHILD** IN TOW.
DEMONS ASSUME HUMAN FORM ALL THE TIME, BUT **HE'S DIFFERENT...** WHEN I LOOK AT HIM, I SEE A HUMAN IN EVERY GESTURE AND NUANCE.
SWOOSH
BUT HIS HUMANITY IS ONLY **SKIN DEEP.** HIS **DEMON ESSENCE** DWELLS **UNSEEN** BELOW THE SURFACE... **THAT** IS WHAT DRAWS ME IRRESISTIBLY TOWARD HIM!

WOOSH

SO YOU'VE FINALLY DECIDED TO SHOW YOURSELF.
BETTER THAT WE MEET ALONE...
SO WE DON'T FRIGHTEN THE LITTLE ONE.
YET, WHEN WAKYO WAS WITH ME YOU DID NOTHING MENACING.
SO HE KNOWS YOU MEAN NO HARM TO HUMANS.
WAKYO? WHO...
AH, YES...THE LITTLE HUMAN IN YOUR THRALL.

NO, YOU ARE QUITE MISTAKEN ...
HE IS ONE OF THEM.

PERHAPS YOU KEEP HIM IN CASE OF EMER-GENCY?
SO WHEN YOU'RE DESPERATE FOR NOURISHMENT YOU CAN NIBBLE A LIMB OR TWO?
THERE'S NO DOUBT!

ENOUGH! THAT'S NOT HOW I TREAT WAKYO!
YES! ANGER!!
RIN PYO TO!
THE DEMON BOILS TO THE SURFACE !!
SHA KAI CHIN RETSU ZAI!

ZEN!
NAU-MAKU-SAM-ANDA BAZ-ARA!
SHOOSH
?!
CLAMP

STOP IT! I JUST WANT TO TALK TO YOU!
CLENCH
WHY ARE YOU DOING THIS? WHY ARE YOU TRYING TO PROVOKE ME?

REMARK-ABLE.
HE RESISTS THE INCAN-TATION!
UGH!
YOU OF ALL DEMONS SHOULD KNOW WHO I AM.

RYOKEI KONO, PRACTIONER OF THE ONMYO ARTS. THEY SAY YOU TRAVEL AMONG THE PEOPLE, DIVINING THE MOTIONS AND SIGNS OF THE HEAVENS.
I REALIZE THAT DEMONS ARE YOUR ENEMIES, BUT I HAVE NEVER--AND I MEAN NEVER--HARMED A HUMAN.

SO YOUR VENDETTA DOES NOT APPLY TO ME.
HMPH

FOOOSH

PFFT
GRAB

SHIIINSH

...IF YOU'RE TRYING TO KILL ME, YOU'RE GOING ABOUT IT ALL WRONG.
HEH
SHIP
I HAVE NO INTENTION OF KILLING YOU.
DROP
SHING
WISE DECI-SION.
SIGH

ANYWAY, I CAN **WAIT** TO **KILL YOU** UNTIL **AFTER GARAI REVEALS HIMSELF.**
TIE UP ALL THE LOOSE ENDS AT ONCE ...
GA...
GARAI ....?

WHAT HAS GARAI DONE?!
I SAID, WHAT HAS HE DONE?
DON'T PRETEND YOU ARE UNAWARE OF YOUR FATHER'S DEEDS!
DO NOT EVEN THINK THAT YOUR FATHER PASSES HIS DAYS WORKING FOR THE GOOD OF THE WORLD, FOR THE GOOD OF HUMANITY, THAT HE-- HOW DID YOU SO SANCTIMONIOUSLY PUT IT?
"HE HAS NEVER EVER HARMED A HUMAN."

GOOOOO
HEAR ME, HOUSE OF KONO-- HEREDITARY FAMILY OF ONMYOJI!
I WARN YOU, DO NOT DARE DEFY ME!
DARLING !! HUSBAND !!
UWAAAH UWAAAH
RUSTLE

?!
H... HEY!
WHAT'S WRONG? CAN YOU STAND?
SO SORRY TO TROUBLE YOU, SOTA.
SOTA?

IT IS SOTA!

NOT AT ALL, MY LADY.
I'M USED TO DEALING WITH CHILDREN.

YOU JUST HURRY AND GET WELL.
HEH!

I BET YOU'RE GLAD YOUR MOM'S OKAY, HM...?
YEAH!
SNUGGLE

THAT SCAR-- WHAT HAPPENED?
THIS?
IT'S FROM A LONG TIME AGO, FROM A FIGHT WITH A POWERFUL DEMON LORD.

OH, FA... FATHER ...!!
SOB! SOB!! SOTA ...!!

UWAAAH
SOTA ...!
AT LEAST THE CHILD WAS SPARED.
I HATE DEMONS I HATE THEM!
THEY ARE A BLIGHT UPON ALL HUMAN-ITY.
RYOTARO, YOU MUST UNDERSTAND.... THE KONO HOUSE-- OUR FAMILY-- EXISTS TO PREVENT OTHERS FROM SUFFERING AS WE DO NOW.

OUR DUTY, OUR MISSION, IS TO VANQUISH THE DEMONS IN OUR MIDST!
...
...
...

WELL? NOW YOU'VE SEEN IT WITH YOUR OWN EYES. HOW CAN YOU DISAGREE?
YOU AND YOUR ILK ARE THE SCOURGE OF HUMAN-ITY.
FWISH
THE ONMYOJI ARE SWORN TO FREE THE WORLD OF DEMON VERMIN LIKE YOU... BISHU!!
FOR SOTA... WE ARE ENEMIES ...!

BOOM!
IT IS OUR LIFE'S WORK! YOU-- MUST-- DIE, BISHU!
WOOOM!
BISHU-SAMA !!

?!
WAKYO!

FOOOSH
UGH ...!
KRAAK
FOOOM

KEEP OUT OF THIS, KID.
MY INCANTATIONS DON'T HARM HUMANS-- BUT THERE'S NO GUARANTEE IF YOU DON'T GET OUT OF THE WAY.

YOU LEAVE BISHU-SAMA ALONE!
WAKYO!
......

FINE ...
BUT UNTIL GARAI'S GONE, REST ASSURED I'M WATCHING YOU.

AND DON'T THINK I'LL PASS UP MY NEXT OPPORTUNITY TO RID THE WORLD OF YOU.

SO MAKE THE MOST OF YOUR LITTLE HUMAN SHIELD WHILE YOU CAN.

DON'T YOU TALK TO BISHU-SAMA LIKE THAT!!
AND YEAH, THAT'S RIGHT-- I PROTECT BISHU-SAMA!

AH ...

BISHU-SAMA...
...ARE YOU ALL RIGHT?

YES, I'M FINE.
THANK YOU, WAKYO.

SOTA...

THE SOTA OF MY CHILDHOOD...

YOUR POWER IS GENTLE AND KIND.
YOU'RE NOT REALLY A DEMON AT ALL, BISHU.

SOTA...
NOW I SEE - GARAI GAVE HIM THOSE SCARS.

KRAAKLE

ALL PRAISE OUR LORD GARAI!
HE'S BEEN BRANDED BY OUR LORD GARAI, YES INDEED.
HEH HEHE
HEAR ME! YOU HAVE INCURRED LORD GARAI'S WRATH!
THE MARK THAT SAYS, "BOIL ME AND FRY ME AND SKIN ME ON A PLANK!"
YOU BEAR THE MARK OF FOOLS WHO DARE DEFY OUR LORD!

THE MARK THAT SAYS, "LORD GARAI HAS LEFT US SOME TASTY SCRAPS TO SATE OUR LUST FOR HUMAN BLOOD!"
SHREEK
EYAAAH
?!

RIIP
SLASH
ZASH
ZASH
SOTA !!

HEEHEE-- HUMAN BLOOD-WINE! DRINK, DRINK!
WATCH THE BLOOD... KILL HIM SLOWLY!
SOTA!
SOTA!
VERMIN! COWARDS!
SNATCH
I AM RYOTARO KONO, THE RIGHTFUL HEIR OF THE KONO HOUSE, PRACTI-TIONERS OF THE ONMYO ARTS!
FIGHT ME, IF YOU DARE, COWARDLY DEMONS!!

AACK
RYO-
TARO
!!
AGH!
ZASH
SNARL
DON'T BE
STUPID!
YOU'RE NO
MATCH FOR
THEM!
SOTA
...!

HO, THE MUNCHKIN SAYS HE WANTS TO PLAY!

AHA HA HA HA

KACKLE

GRUNT

SO SORRY NOT TO PLAY! BLOOD AND ENTRAILS, CRACKLING BONES AND HUMAN GROANS, ARE WHAT BRINGS US HERE TODAY.

RYOTARO -- RUN!!

SOTA!

AHA HA HA!

SLIIIITHER
UGH --!
SOTA ?!

SOTA ?!
NOW SIT WE DOWN TO EAT GARAI-SAMA'S GRACIOUS TREAT!!
HAR HAR HAR HAR
SOTA! SOTA!!
WHAT'S WRONG? WHY CAN'T YOU MOVE?

IS IT YOUR WOUND ...?!
RYO... RUN... PLEASE ...
SPLORP

SOTA ...!!

SOTA! SOTA!!
SOTA---!!
THIS IS **HIS** DOING!
YOU DID THIS...
...TO SOTA!!

GASP
GARAI !!
HUFF HUFF
UGH ...
PAIN
GARAI ...

STUPID BOY ... ...BLAMING GARAI-SAMA FOR YOUR MIS-FORTUNE.

!!
ALLOW ME TO TELL YOU WHAT REALLY HAPPENED.

ALL DEMONS ARE LIARS. WHY SHOULD I BELIEVE YOU?
SUIT YOURSELF...
BUT THIS IS ALL BISHU'S DOING!
...?!
WHAT?
SOTA HIMSELF SAID SO, DIDN'T HE?
"KEEPING A CHILD OUT OF HARM'S WAY"--

CHILD ...?
YESSS... CHILD! NONE OTHER THAN BISHU, SON OF THE DEMON LORD YOU FIND SO REPUL-SIVE.
SOTA'S DEATH WAS THE DOING OF FATHER AND SON--?
YES! YESSS ...!

FATHER AND SON, YES...BUT NEVER DOUBT WHO IS THE TRUE AUTHOR OF THIS CALAMITY!
BISHU! YESSS, BISHU-- HE IS THE PUPPET MASTER!!
PIECES OF A SPIRAL 6 END

PIECES OF A SPIRAL
螺旋のかけら
らせん
SHORT STORY - MAYUKO

ACE of WANDS
TELL, MAYUKO, TELL ...!
HMM, A SEVEN OF PENTACLES.

LUCKY YOU.
IN THE FIRST POSITION IT INDICATES POTENTIAL-- USEFUL TALENTS, ABILITIES, AND SKILLS.
WOW! OH, THANK YOU, THANK YOU, MA-YUKO!
BUT BE SURE TO USE YOUR TALENTS WISELY, OKAY?
BASICALLY, IT MEANS YOUR HARD WORK WILL BE WELL RE-WARDED.
OKAY!
DO ME NEXT, MAYUKO!
NO, ME!

WOW, EVERY BREAK SHE DRAWS A TOTAL CROWD.
WHAT DO YOU EXPECT? KAKEI'S FORTUNES ARE NEVER WRONG.
HORO-SCOPES, CHINESE ASTROLOGY, FORTUNE TELLING, TAROT CARDS... SHE DOES IT ALL.
SHE'S A REAL PROPH-ET!
SO, MAYUKO ...
YOU EVER DO YOUR OWN FORTUNE?
MC
DEC
SURE.
I CAN DO MY HOROSCOPE AND CHINESE ASTROLOGY BECAUSE ALL THEY NEED IS A DATE OF BIRTH.

BUT *TAROT* AND *FORTUNE TELLING* HAVE TOO MUCH RANDOMNESS-- IT STIRS UP THE *SUBCONSCIOUS.*
AND FOR *ME*...

IT'S LIKE... TELLING A *STRANGER'S* FORTUNE.

WHAT DO YOU *MEAN, MAYUKO?*

SIGH...

I MEAN, IT SHOULD BE MY FORTUNE, BUT IT'S NOT--IT'S SOMEONE ELSE'S.
?
HUH? MAYUKO, I DON'T GET IT.

WHAT'S THE *MATTER* WITH ME?! LISTEN TO ME *BABBLE AWAY.*
WE HAVE *FOR-TUNES* TO TELL!

JUST FIVE BUCKS !!!
FIVE EACH, THAT IS!
HUUUUH!!

SQUEAK
......
IT ALL BEGAN WHEN I STARTED DIVINATION.

EYEEEW ...!
HEY, WHAT'S UP?
GET AWAY FROM ME!!
UGH, AND IT'S WHY I SEE CREEPY VERMIN LIKE THAT!
KLANK

THEY ARE DEMONS ESCAPED FROM BISHU'S THRALL COME TO HARM HUMANS.

WHAT?
WHO SAID THAT?

GASP -- IT WAS ME?!?
REALLY? WELL, WHEN YOU WERE LITTLE YOU'D HAVE IMAGINARY CONVERSATIONS ALL THE TIME.
WE WORRIED YOU MIGHT HAVE A SPLIT PERSONALITY.

A SPLIT PERSONALITY?

BUT RIGHT AROUND KINDERGARTEN...
YOU WERE SUCH A SOLEMN CHILD.
IT JUST SUDDENLY STOPPED.

MAYBE IT'S BACK-- YOUR "SPLIT PERSONALITY."

...
STARE
SHOULD WE SEE A DOCTOR?

C'MON, LET'S NOT GET CRAZY! I DON'T HAVE A SPLIT PERSONALITY!
WELL, I HOPE YOU'RE RIGHT.

SO, I'VE GOT A SPLIT PERSONALITY...
IT'S CERTAINLY NO LAUGHING MATTER.

WHENEVER I DO MY OWN FORTUNE...
IT'S LIKE ANOTHER PERSON JUST COMES OUT OF NOWHERE.

I CAN'T FIGURE IT OUT...

IF IT'S NOT MY PAST...

WHOSE IS IT? AND WHEN?

ALL I KNOW IS THAT IT REACHES BACK TO THE DIMMEST EDGE OF MY MEMORY TO A TIME VERY, VERY LONG AGO...

IF YOU *WERE* REINCAR-NATED, *NOW* WOULD BE THE *TIME*.
BISHU, WHERE *ARE* YOU?

YOU'RE NOT BREAKING YOUR PROMISE TO ME, ARE YOU, BISHU?
BISHU ...

HEY! WHO'S THERE ?!
MORNING ...!
TOTALLY EXHAUSTED...
SO SLEEPY.
?
STAAAAARE...

WH ...
WHAT'S EVERY-BODY *LOOKING* AT...?
KLUNK
TWO SLICES, PLEASE
MAYUKO... WHERE DID YOU *GO* LAST NIGHT?
HUH? WHERE'D I *GO?*

DOES A *PROPER* YOUNG LADY *LEAVE HOME* IN THE *MIDDLE OF THE NIGHT WITHOUT TELLING HER PARENTS?*
WHAT?
DEAR, YOU NEED TO *GET GOING* ...
YES.

YOU KNOW YOUR DAD'S TRANS-FERRING TO THE NEW YORK OFFICE, MAYUKO.
WE HAVE ENOUGH TO WORRY ABOUT RIGHT NOW.
Y-YEAH, OKAY, DAD ...

MAYUKO, YOU HURRY UP, TOO, OR YOU'RE GOING TO BE LATE!

WAIT--I REMEM-BER ...!
SORRY-- I CAN'T GO TO SCHOOL TODAY-- I'M SICK!
BAM
MA-YUKO ?!
YES, I REMEMBER NOW!

SHUFFLE
I DID GO OUT LAST NIGHT--!
IT WASN'T A DREAM !!
THIS IS TOO WEIRD... WHAT'S HAPPENING TO ME ?!

IT DOESN'T WORK -- I CAN'T DO MY OWN FOR-TUNE ...!
WHAM
THE STAR
WHAT IS HAPPENING TO ME?!
CALM DOWN, ALL RIGHT? YOUR HEART'S BEATING FIT TO BURST.
?!
SIGH
I WASN'T IMAGINING IT--THERE IS ANOTHER PERSON INSIDE ME--
ANOTHER... PERSON...?

TWO of SWORDS
NOT QUITE...
NO...
THE MOON
TWO of WANDS
BUT A SECOND CONSCIOUS-NESS AS REAL AND DISTINCT AS MY OWN...

MAYUKO! YOU'RE FEELING *BETTER?*
YUP, I FEEL *FINE.*
AH YES, NOW IT IS *CRYSTAL CLEAR...*

WHAT I DO...
WHAT I THINK...
MY PAST LIVES...
RIN PYO TO--
ALL MY KARMA ...
YES ...!

NOW THE SEARCH BEGINS ...
ZEN!
THE SEARCH FOR THE DEMON LORD CHILD WITH THE GLITTERING VIOLET EYES.

FOR I HAVE A MISSION TO FULFILL AND A PROMISE TO KEEP TO BISHU ...!
MAYUKO / END

AFTERWORD

HI! IT'S ME, KAIMU! I SOOO WANT TO GET OUT AND ABOUT. IT'S THE PERFECT TIME OF YEAR FOR BEING OUTSIDE, WHAT WITH THE CHERRY BLOSSOMS AND ALL. BUT THERE'S NO TIME! MAYBE I'LL AT LEAST JUMP IN THE CAR AND GO SOMEWHERE NICE. HERE IT IS! PIECES OF A SPIRAL VOLUME 6. CAN YOU BELIEVE IT? SIX VOLUMES SO FAR AND I OWE IT ALL TO YOU, MY LOYAL READERS. THIS TIME AROUND I HAD A PILE OF REVISIONS, BUT I THINK IT TURNED OUT ALL RIGHT, AND ANYWAY I WANT TO STAY ON SCHEDULE FOR VOLUME 7 ?SO BE KIND TO ME AS YOU READ. GUESS WHAT? I FINALLY WENT OUT AND GOT A DVD PLAYER. I GUESS THE NEXT STEP IS TO GO OUT AND BUY A PILE OF DVDS? EVEN THOUGH THE PLAYER'S STILL IN ITS BOX! AND TO MAKE A SPOT FOR IT, TOO, BECAUSE RIGHT NOW MY ROOM IS IN THE SAME SORRY STATE AS MAYUKO'S!

PROBLEM NO. 1

ANYWAY, I HAVE TO CLEAN UP MY PLACE AND MAKE A SPOT FOR THE PLAYERS SOMEWHERE!
MAYBE A CREW OF KINDLY PIXIES WILL DO IT FOR ME WHILE I'M ASLEEP...
SO, IN THIS EPISODE, RUKI PAID THE ULTIMATE PRICE.
BUT MY ASSISTANT STILL DOESN'T WANT TO BELIEVE IT--MAYBE HE'LL COME TO LIFE.
GUESS I'LL NEED TO DO SOMETHING TO CONVINCE EVERYBODY THAT HE'S NOT COMING BACK--THAT THIS IS FOR KEEPS!
LATELY, I SEEM TO BE REALLY PUTTING MY CHARACTERS THROUGH THE WRINGER--EVERY OTHER PAGE SEEMS TO HAVE BUCKETS OF BLOOD-TONE.
SO WHO'S GONNA GET THE BLOOD TONE TREATMENT NEXT VOLUME, I WONDER...?
THAT'S FOR US ALL TO FIND OUT IN VOLUME 7.
SO BACK TO WORK AND BYE FOR NOW!

KAIMU

Glenn Rich – Translation and Adaptation
Ryan Cline – Lettering
Larry Berry – Design
Jim Chadwick – Editor

ISBN:1-4012-1032-5
ISBN-13: 13: 978-1-4012-1032-8